C000096614

Barnet

IN OLD PHOTOGRAPHS

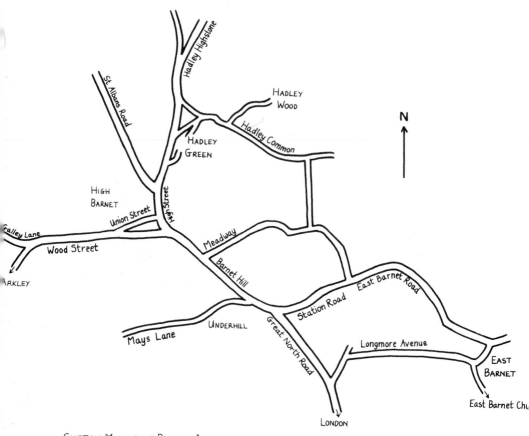

Hadley Highstone

St Albans Road

HADLEY
WOOD

Hadley Common

HADLEY
GREEN

N

HIGH
BARNET

High Street

Union Street

Calley Lane

Wood Street

Meadway

ARKLEY

Barnet Hill

East Barnet Road

Station Road

UNDERHILL

Mays Lane

Great North Road

Longmore Avenue

EAST
BARNET

East Barnet Chu

LONDON

Sketch Map of the Barnet Area

Barnet

IN OLD PHOTOGRAPHS

Compiled by IAN NORRIE

With the co-operation of the
Barnet and District Local History
Society

ALAN
SUTTON

Alan Sutton Publishing Limited
Phoenix Mill · Far Thrupp
Stroud · Gloucestershire

First Published 1993

British Library Cataloguing
in Publication Data

Norrie, Ian
    Barnet in Old Photographs
    I. Title
    942.187

    ISBN 0-7509-0291-4

Typeset in 9/10 Sabon.
Typesetting and origination by
Alan Sutton Publishing Limited.
Printed in Great Britain by
Redwood Books, Trowbridge.

Copyright © Ian Norrie 1993

The Barnet town silver prize band in 1921 with supporters' club in the back row.

Contents

	Acknowledgements and Bibliography	6
	Introduction	7
1.	Hill and Underhill	9
2.	Fair and Market	37
3.	High Street and Environs	47
4.	Wood Street to Arkley	75
5.	The Hadleys	93
6.	East Barnet, New Barnet	115
7.	War	141
8.	Sport and Customs	151

Acknowledgements and Bibliography

I am most grateful to the officers and committee of the Barnet and District Local History Society for sanctioning access to their archives, photographic and otherwise, without which it would have been impossible for me to compile and write this book. I particularly wish to thank John Heathfield, curator of the Barnet Museum and also chairman of the Society. He was totally, good humouredly cooperative over many months when I leant upon his goodwill, knowledge and time. He was always available to answer queries, institute research and write informative notes for my guidance, often in the intervals of delivering lectures and performing to classes of schoolchildren and teachers visiting the Museum. In his presence local history is always lively, which is exactly how it should be. On occasions W.H. (Bill) Gelder was also present and I was able to draw on his lifelong experience of Barnet. I deeply appreciate the interest and friendship which John, Bill, Doug Austin and other members of the Society extended to me.

Almost all the photographs are reproduced by permission of the Barnet and District Local History Society in whose archives the originals are held. Individual photographers are seldom known. Where they are the name is usually given in the relevant caption, but I wish to acknowledge the photographs of F.W. Peters (pp. 32, 33, 68), A.G. Chivers (p. 46), E. Daws (pp. 122, 126), J.M. Dyer (p. 87), W. Dyer (p. 75), and E.W. Reeve (p. 101). I must also thank Edward and Nancy Blishen (pp. 88, 138), Charles Rose (p. 139) and W. Harding Young (p. 46) for the loan of prints, and Percy Reboul who spent many days making prints from the original Museum photographs.

The definitive history of Barnet has yet to be written. Comparatively little has been published about the town in book form although in the Museum archives there is material enough for a dozen or more large volumes. I delved into many impeccably organized cabinets to seek and find information, and also into the following books.

Barnet and District Local History Society, *60 Years of Local History, 1927-1987*.

W.H. Gelder, *Georgian Hadley*, Barnet Press Group, 1974.

W.H. Gelder (ed.), *Historic Barnet*, Muir's Bookshop, 1984.

Pevsner, Nikolaus and Cherry, Bridget, *The Buildings of England: Hertfordshire*, Penguin, rev. 1977.

S.H. Widdicombe, *A Chat about Barnet and its History*, privately published by the Barnet Press, 1912.

In addition I consulted several of the Bulletins issued by the Local History Society.

Ian Norrie

Introduction

First define your Barnet.

At the Conquest the heavily forested territory fifteen miles north of Westminster lay in the domain of the Abbot of St Albans and was sparsely populated with only a woodcutter and a swineherd or two. The abbot did not support William of Normandy, which cost him his lands closer to London, but according to the *Domesday Book* (1086), the abbey still owned sizeable chunks of Hertfordshire twenty years later, though Barnet is not specifically mentioned. And more than a century after (1199) a charter of King John awarded the abbot's successors the right of a market there. In the first Manorial Roll of 1245 the town is referred to as 'la Barnet' with the manor house and parish church being then at East Barnet. It was not until the nineteenth century that East and Chipping (High) Barnet became separate parishes with New Barnet also establishing itself parochially in 1899.

North of Barnet lies Monken Hadley which once had a priory that was an outpost, not of St Albans, but of Saffron Walden. On one side of it were Hadley Green and Highstone, on another, Hadley Common. In 1471 its peace was disturbed when the penultimate battle of the Wars of the Roses was fought nearby in mist and confusion. Evidence of a more tranquil past is to be found in Green and Common, described by Nikolaus Pevsner as 'one of the most felicitous pictures of Georgian town planning'. One ancient boundary between Hadley and Barnet is found in the latter's High Street, emphasizing the tie between the two.

Until 1965, Chipping Barnet and East Barnet were independent urban district councils incorporating parts of Hadley. Following the creation of the Greater London Council (now defunct) Barnet acquired a wider orbit encompassing most of what had been in the urban districts mentioned above plus Finchley, Friern Barnet and Hendon, including Burnt Oak and the Hampstead Garden Suburb. This overlarge creation of municipally contrived geography has never captured the popular imagination, and why should it? It was imposed for political reasons which backfired on the instigators. Residents of Chipping, East and New Barnets may be content with the designation of their Greater London Borough but others, remote from the height to which it owes its name, probably are not.

So the Barnet of this book is Chipping, East, New, but not Friern. Nor is it Finchley, Hendon, Totteridge, Whetstone, Burnt Oak, etc., though it does include the Hadleys and Arkley. They, with the three Barnets, are homogeneous, belonging together in, on and around the hill which, you might think in all historical decency, should be crowned with at least the vestiges of a castle. There never was one, nor was the church ever fortified.

Barnet Hill, with its market, and the twice yearly livestock fair chartered by Elizabeth I in 1588, was the making of the community. The Romans found their way from Londinium to Verulamium along Watling Street, bypassing Barnet which doesn't, therefore, have any recorded history until centuries after

St Albans boasted an abbey. Then, in 1690, when the favoured way north ignored Watling Street, Chipping Barnet became a stage on the route with numerous inns catering for more than the crowds drawn to the famous fairs.

In time better roads were demanded. Levels were lowered here, heightened there, and the actual route on the hillside changed from a circuitous track on the south side to an almost straight thoroughfare on the eastern approach. It was justified in the cause of progress but had scarcely been achieved before the Railway Age dawned. Not, though, on Barnet.

The locomotive entrepreneurs, like the Romans, sought a way round the hill. Complicated schemes were formulated for encircling Barnet but the main track was laid, in 1850, through what became New Barnet and Hadley Wood. It was not until 1871 that the Great Northern Company brought a rail head to the township on the hill, except that it placed the buffers well down the slope. In 1940, London Transport took over at the same level for one of the termini of its 'underground' system. The station is named, ironically, *High* Barnet.

By then road transport had long since entered a new phase with electric trams grinding their way up the wide hill to the site of the original market by the church. And cars had become more reliable so that traffic on the Great North Road was busier than ever before. Increasingly powerful trucks, replacing horse-drawn transport, required petrol not forage, and soon there was a demand for wider, faster arteries.

Once again, Barnet was bypassed, and ceased to be a staging post. Instead it became a dormitory suburb with most of the freight traffic eventually diverted on to motorways. It had another advantage; it was on the edge of green belt. Unlike Finchley, Hendon, Burnt Oak, it overlooked fields, copses, farmland and, although there have been encroachments, it is still apparent that London ends here. Long may this be so.

How much the past matters depends on what you notice as you walk about. If you are a commuter from lowly positioned High Barnet station, what do you see as you hasten down the steep footpath to buffer level? What do you observe as you puff up the same gradient ten, twelve hours later?

History is only alive in old photographs if you relate them to what you see in your daily peregrinations. It would require the imagination of a major novelist to envisage the High Street as Queen Elizabeth I may have seen it when she journeyed to and from Hatfield House; it is less difficult to visualize the more recent past. Photography is an aid to folk memory and perusal of the shots published here will assist the remembrance of things past.

The Barnets and Arkley have grown and changed; four of the Hadleys are less altered. The photographs I have chosen illustrate the past from 30 to 110 years ago. Except in a few instances I have not included buildings which are still standing unless their use, appearance and surroundings have changed. Making the choice provoked agonies of indecision. A few have appeared in other publications but, as a whole, this selection is unique and is presented here in the belief that old photographs prove that history is not bunk.

SECTION ONE ·

Hill and Underhill

This section covers Barnet Hill as far as Church Passage where the road turns northwards into the flat part of the High Street. The street numbering is continuous with the Hill taken as part of the High. The King's Head (above, *c.* 1880) was at No. 84. To its right is the site of the old Red Lion visited by Samuel Pepys. It later became the Assembly Room and then the Barnet Theatre which closed in 1837. A few doors down today there is again a theatre, the Old Bull.

The tram terminus at Barnet church, August 1933.

The first electric tram reached Barnet on Good Friday, 1907. Intending passengers queueing for the return journey to London.

Church Passage, *c.* 1900. The Hyde Institute
(public library) was built to the left of the
photograph. Note from the advertisement (right)
how Joseph Baughen diversified – not only
carpenter, decorator and undertaker but also
upholsterer.

ESTABLISHED UPWARDS OF FIFTY YEARS.

JOSEPH BAUGHEN,

BUILDER,

DECORATOR, AND UNDERTAKER,

CHURCH PASSAGE, BARNET.

The Strictest Personal attention given in all Branches of
the Business.

*All kinds of Furniture Cleaned and Repaired.
Old Mattresses Re-made equal to New.*

CARPETS MADE AND FITTED TO ANY ROOM.

J. B., having had 25 years' practical experience, trusts to merit
a continuance of past favours and support.

ALL COMMUNICATIONS TO BE ADDRESSED TO

CHURCH PASSAGE, BARNET.

Middle Row in 1889. While it stood there was no clear view of the parish church of St John for travellers up Barnet Hill. Shops and homes were not actually adjuncts to the nave and apse, as with many French churches, but formed an island where once the market was held. Is the demure little lady awaiting a conveyance to the Silesian College in Bell's Hill, named on the signpost above her?

Middle Row and 'the bottle neck', facing east, after the fire in 1889 (see p. 14).

The fenced-in bakery was named Fortescue.

Mummery, who diversified even more widely than Baughen, faced the east end of the parish church in Middle Row. The fire which destroyed his premises on 17 June 1889 was caused by an oil lamp overturning. In the top picture opposite policemen and a dog guard the charred ruins. The entire obstruction to the church was demolished in the early 1890s before the lower photograph was taken. This shows Pearson, grocer, and Wm. Friday, butcher and poulterer, in what remains today the narrowest part of the High Street.

W.E. Payne, on the south side of the hill, at Nos 39–41, *c.* 1891. The left-hand part of the shop is now the Café au Lait.

Gentle was at No. 43 at a much later date than Payne. His van is seen outside the Highstone Teashop at Hadley.

Barnet church after Middle Row's removal, showing its enlarged status (by William Butterfield) and the metal flèche by J.C. Traylen (1893).

J.A. Clark & Son opened in 1870 and remained until 1985. Many residents recall the steep, wide steps to its lower floor which defied entry to invalid carriages and pushchairs. Some of the headgear shown here during Empire Shopping Week (early twenties) is housed in the Barnet Museum. The site is now the Barnet Food Hall.

TO BUILDERS, SPECULATORS, AND OTHERS.

BARNET, HERTS

Situated in an elevated position about 400 feet above sea level; on the Great North Road, along which the Middlesex and Hertfordshire Electric Tramway (Highgate to Barnet) passes; at the summit of Barnet Hill and at the southern entrance of the Town; immediately opposite High Barnet Station on the G.N.R. and about 15 minutes from New Barnet Station on the G.N.R. (Main Line).

NOTICE OF SALE BY AUCTION OF

27 FREEHOLD SHOP SITES

— AND —

104 FREEHOLD BUILDING PLOTS

Occupying eligible and choice positions in

NORMANDY AVENUE AND BEDFORD AVENUE,

"LAWN HOUSE ESTATE," BARNET,

HERTS.

Ripe for erection of Good-class Shops and Detached and Semi-Detached Villa Residences for which there is a good steady demand.

Which

Messrs. CHARLES

SPARROW & SON

Have been favoured with instructions to offer by public Auction at the

RED LION HOTEL, BARNET,

On MONDAY, the 6th of JULY, 1908,

At SEVEN o'clock, precisely.

Particulars, Plan, and Conditions of Sale may be obtained at the place of Sale; of the

or of the   Vendor's Solicitors: Messrs. BARFIELD & BARFIELD, 17, Finsbury Square, London, E.C.;

Auctioneers and Surveyors: Messrs. CHARLES SPARROW & SON, North Finchley and

Below, houses in Bedford Avenue, *c.* 1910, perhaps built as a result of this advertisement. Normandy and Bedford Avenues were laid out after the railhead had been established at High Barnet.

1447.   Bedford Avenue Barnet.

Inns close to the top of the hill, all popular in the heyday of coaching. The Red Lion (above, around 1880) is now less extensive and named The Dandy Lion. At the Mitre (below) Gen. Monck stayed in 1660. It dates from around 1540. The Woolpack (opposite) surrendered its licence in 1931. The trees and horse trough have long since gone.

Fitzjohn Avenue, *c.* 1910. Nowadays parked cars and traffic preclude street games.

Mrs Ashley at the door of her Northaw Charity bungalow (*c.* 1911–15), when it was about to be sold. It was one of four cottages, standing near The Woolpack, built with funds provided by James I.

Postal delivery at Nickolds, No. 88 High Street, opposite the churchyard.

Mr Smith (extreme right) and staff outside his general store at Nos 60–2 High Street, *c*. 1896. The manager wears a bowler. All but Smith wear long aprons to protect their clothing. Almost certainly the assistants owned only one pair of working trousers each.

H. Sinclair was a greengrocer here, on the corner of Park Road, until the bank was built in 1892. Below is the Westminster Bank (now Natwest) in 1967, a few doors above the police station, which has since been rebuilt.

Barnet Hill, *c.* 1896, with the old police station on extreme right. Below the recently erected bank (see p. 25) is another, the London and County Bank, with a handsome first-floor bay.

Barnet Police Force including plain-clothes officers, *c.* 1910.

The old police station, *c.* 1880.

The original Victoria Cottage Hospital was on the site of the present Queen Elizabeth's Girls' School, facing a path, now Meadway, to New Barnet.

James Hill, Gentleman, at the door of his house in 1860. Like the grand residence with Dutch gables and stone mullioned windows, it later became classrooms for Queen Elizabeth's Girls' School.

Barnet Hill, *c.* 1880. The scene is unrecognizable to present-day citizens, because the fields seen here have long been smothered by urban sprawl. Yet stretches of land to the right, towards Totteridge, are still, if not open country, at least countrified, as anyone living in flats near the county boundary at Willenhall will testify. In the scene depicted, immediately to the right of the railway bridge (centre) can be discerned Underhill House and Underhill Farm (see p. 34). On the left of the bridge is a large semi-detached property, probably on the site of the fire station erected in the early 1990s.

Carnival procession ascending the hill, 5 July 1923.

Shunting accident, August 1953, when a Northern Line train was derailed perilously close to the old Great North Road. No one was hurt.

The Queen's Arms at the approach to Barnet Hill near the entrance to Potters Lane. The lower picture advertises petrol but does not show the pub trying to attract cyclists. Both views date from between 1900 and 1905.

The Great North Road. Barnet.

The 'old' Old Red Lion was a cottage alehouse in the early eighteenth century during which it was enlarged to become, by 1789, 'a very bad inn with a dirty puzzle-headed Irish waiter', according to one Viscount Torrington. At the corner of Barnet Lane, it was well-sited for traffic up the old lane to the hill top, but when this was bypassed by the new road (1827), the inn lost much of its trade.

The 'new' Old Red Lion, here seen in 1934, was replaced by the present building in 1952. (Neither should be confused with other Red Lions up the hill.) This one, and its predecessor, the 'old' Old Red Lion became convenient refreshment points for visitors to the fair at Underhill and for supporters of Barnet Football Club.

Underhill House, 1932, when it had been unoccupied for five years. The Daws family lived here during its last years. It is now the cinema site.

Whitehall (formerly Underhill) Farm, 1932. Built about 1820, it lay to the south of Underhill House.

This barn was part of Sharp's Farm, in Mays Lane, near the bottom of Fitzjohn Avenue, close to the ill-conceived Dollis Brook Estate. It was demolished in the 1970s.

Sharp's Farm in better fettle, probably, in this instance, seen in mid-First World War.

Leeside Works, Mays Lane, *c.* 1925, looking like an army camp. Dawkins & Co. manufactured strings here for musical instruments.

SECTION TWO

Fair and Market

This is believed to be Joseph Berriman, at 85, lessee and 'father' of Barnet Fair, who died at Finsbury Park, 23 December 1930. He inherited a 'prescriptive right' to run the Fair and for over sixty years he took a lease on the fairground, subletting stands and exacting a toll for each animal put on sale.

The 1588 charter laid down the dates of the twice yearly Fair as 23–25 June and 17–19 October to coincide with certain saints' days, but by the eighteenth century April and September became the preferred months. The venue has changed many times and there were frequent objections to the Fair being held at all because it was supposed to generate public disorder. Among those who fought successfully against closure, at different times, were W. Osborn Boyes, W.E. Boyes and Walter Wright, solicitors of Wood Street, and town clerk, Alfred S. Mays. They and others understood what prosperity and colour it brought to Barnet. The horse pictured above (around 1925) is expressing its dissatisfaction with the Fair.

Cartoon from the *Pictorial World*, 1883, when the Fair was held at Underhill.

The 1913 Barnet Fair held off Mays Lane.

Print from the *Illustrated London News*, 1848, when the Fair was held on Barnet Common, which covered land on both sides of Wood Street. The buildings in the distance are Whitings Hill Farm.

A spirited Welsh pony at Barnet Fair in September 1928.

A horse striving successfully for attention, *c.* 1910.

The Fair of 1905 held at the foot of Barnet Hill.

The 1937 Fair held off Barnet Lane close to the playing fields.

Pleasure as well as business on the slopes of Underhill, *c* . 1910.

General William Booth, founder of the Salvation Army, addressing a gathering in the market, *c.* 1908, four years before his death aged 83. Gen. Booth lived in nearby Hadley Wood where there is a plaque to him. The *Dictionary of National Biography* says of him that '[he] probably changed more lives for better than any other religious emotionalist for centuries'.

A nicely posed shot of eager marketeers about to take advantage of 'Tip Top Quality at Rock Bottom Prices', *c.* 1920.

The cattle market on 8 December 1909, sited between Bruce Road and Chipping Close. Bruce Road, now severely truncated, once joined Stapylton Road.

W. Harding Young presiding over one of the last auctions in the cattle market in the 1950s. He was a partner in Harlands, the High Street estate agents which acquired the rights in the livestock market in 1849. Now in his eighties, Mr Young still takes an active interest in the Barnet Stall Market which took over from the livestock in 1960. It is held twice weekly.

SECTION THREE

High Street and Environs

The High Street, *c.* 1910. The Spires was still then the frontage of the Methodist church, not the entrance to a shopping precinct. Note, on the right, T.C. Grosvenor, chemist, on the site of what is now Boots. This is still the boundary between the parishes of Chipping Barnet and Hadley.

The Salisbury Arms, *c.* 1895, when the licensee was G. Toone. The lady fifth from the left is Minnie Toone. This was an official meeting place for cyclists who were served tea, not alcohol, Minnie being an early advocate of Don't Drink and Drive.

The Salisbury, then a hotel, rebuilt in 1927 in mock-Tudor style and decorated for a royal occasion. Demolished in 1988, this is now the site of Iceland.

Nos 116–18 High Street, *c.* 1948. Note, above Mulhollands, Maison Elaine, offering 'Machineless Permalotte luxury perms'.

High Street, *c.* 1900, looking south with part of the old post office on the extreme left.

Fire gutted premises above the Home and Colonial Stores in 1934 and temporarily closed the Barnet Cinema.

A notice says the Barnet Cinema, which was only smoke-damaged, will reopen on Monday.

Woolworths, now the site of the Abbey National, soon to open, 1935. On the left, Boots has already replaced T.C. Grosvenor (see p. 47).

The Star Hotel, No. 108 High Street, 1933. It closed in 1959.

Pulham's, butchers, at No. 148 High Street, has flags out to celebrate a visit by Prince (later King) George, November 1932.

The Salisbury Arms decorated for the Armistice, 1918.

Three shops burned to the ground in two hours in this 1908 conflagration. Shortage of water was blamed. Later W.H. Smith was here for many decades until removing to the Spires in 1993.

The scene after the fire, with the stonework of Barclays Bank on the corner of Salisbury Road at extreme right. The bank was unharmed.

Mary Payne's Place (above), *c.* 1920; and (below) Place and stalls facing what is now St Albans Road, *c.* 1928.

Mary Payne's Place in 1933, Nos 166–72 High Street. This is almost identical as a terrace with its appearance today but the shops have different names. Mary's husband, Matthew Benjamin, acquired the site early in the nineteenth century. Her Place, Nos 1–14, on three sides of a rectangle, included cottages and a gasworks. On her son's death in 1874 it was bought by Daniel Schmidt, tailor. The area where the shops now stand seems, from the top photograph opposite, to have been used as an *ad hoc* stall market.

Pedder's, High Street, 1882. Pedder's was a corn and flour merchant, also a granary and dairy, trading where Dolcis stands now. A notice advertises, 'Best clover and clean chaff'.

E.J. Wills recorded the High Street on film between 1946 and 1950. Of the businesses shown here, situated at Nos 178–202, all have changed hands or use, apart from Robinson's popular delicatessen which has successfully survived into the supermarket era. No. 190 is still a pharmacy (Wilkinsons), but is no longer obsessed with advertising Meggezones (top picture opposite). The Little Gem (bottom opposite) was a confectioner selling 'the sweets we remember having as children'. It was here until the early 1970s. Wynne's next door became Muir's Bookshop.

The funeral cortège of Chief Fire Officer C.F. Norton passing the junction with St Albans Road, then New Road, 1931.

The so-called Corn Exchange shortly before demolition. Its 1891 replacement, for long a branch of Williams Brothers (seen behind the funeral procession opposite), is still there, occupied by Kall-Kwik printers. (The Exchange was in fact one firm of corn dealers, E. & J. Eldred.)

High Street facing south, c. 1890. Seen from the Corn Exchange with the Wellington and Old Green Dragon pubs on the right.

Grove House, seen here in 1910, stood back from the High Street at the Hadley end on what is now Grove Court. This handsome early nineteenth-century house became a tea place in the 1920s.

West side of the High Street, 1935, taken from the first-floor window of No. 128, then A.J. Wills, grocer.

Pupils of Moxon Street School, *c.* 1903. The school, which they are facing, is now the British Legion's local headquarters. The house behind them has gone. It is now a car park.

The Old Rising Sun in the 1890s, next to Bennetts the butchers. It was rebuilt in the 1940s but demolished a decade later.

Bennetts, on the corner of Union Street, which became an off-licence in 1950.

Nos 67–71 High Street before 1885. The site was developed as the present post office early in the twentieth century.

The earlier post office at No. 122 High Street, *c.* 1890. Does this record a lock out? Or are these stage postmen about to burst into song?

The High Street decorated for the coronation of George VI, 1937. Nunneley & Son, drapers, is now split between the British Gas showrooms and a hairdressers.

Nos 103–7 High Street, probably in the 1930s, between Barracks Lane and the Spires.

High Street, looking north, *c.* 1930. Note the casual attitude of the two gentlemen (one wearing plus-fours) standing chatting in the road.

The Co-op shop in Salisbury Road, *c.* 1895. It adjoined the Salvation Army Citadel which was opened by Commandant and Mrs T. Booth on 20 March 1891. The building was recently demolished and the site remains empty. The former CWS premises house a charity shop and an insurance company.

Corner of Union Street and High Street, September 1934, showing Chas. Baker's extensive premises. By 1961 Hope Bros. were trading here in similar merchandise. The corner unit only is now Clark's shoeshop.

Gladwin's head office was at No. 11 Union Street; Ogles were rope dealers at No. 186 High Street.

The Albion, Union Street, 1931, long known popularly as 'de Vos's' from the name of the licensee. Beyond is the Roman Catholic church destroyed by fire in June 1973.

The Assembly Hall, Union Street, October 1930, later used as Labour Party headquarters. It is now Longrove Surgery.

The former Barnet Town Hall in Union Street, projecting a mean image, when compared with the elegance of East Barnet's premises in Station Road (see pp. 130–31). This centre of municipal life and strife became a printing works and is now named Century House with several occupants.

William Druce's thatched home and workplace in Coe's Alley, now Nos 65–73 Union Street. The board reads:

> William Druce here does dwell
> Grinds razors, knives and scissors well.
> There's very few can him excel
> In mending pots and kettles well.

NB Umbrellas and parasols recovered and repaired on the shortest notice.

Mrs Druce's sweet shop was also here; she was renowned for her toffee-making.

The former premises of Messrs Wm. Cutbush & Son awaiting replacement by the present drill hall, 1937, in New Road, now St Albans Road.

Cover of the Cutbush catalogue for autumn, 1879.

Bruce Road, probably 1930. The sign above and to the left of The Egg Shop reads, HORSES FORAGED BY CONTRACT. Linton's in New Road, is now Hammersleys, independent fishmongers.

W.S. Slough, builder, lived in Byng Road and was active until the 1920s. His horse and cart are seen here, in 1915, in New Road.

The 84 bus (the route survives although it now goes through Potters Bar) passing the Green Dragon in the 1920s.

Boys in Alston Road, c. 1910. The oak tree has gone but the pub in the background, The Sebright Arms, remains.

1st Barnet Scout Troop marching along the High Street, 1913. The occasion is not recorded, a minor one perhaps, because only a single flag is draped from an upper window. How many of those who marched survived the horror soon to come?

SECTION FOUR

Wood Street to Arkley

The Tudor Hall of Barnet Grammar School was built about 1573. In the 1920s, when the wisteria grew over it, it was part of Queen Elizabeth's Boys' School, but it has since been incorporated into Barnet College.

The Tudor Hall was still used as a classroom in the 1920s.

Some appealing anarchy of costume here. Master and boys at Queen Elizabeth's around 1890–5, before the tyranny of school uniform ruled.

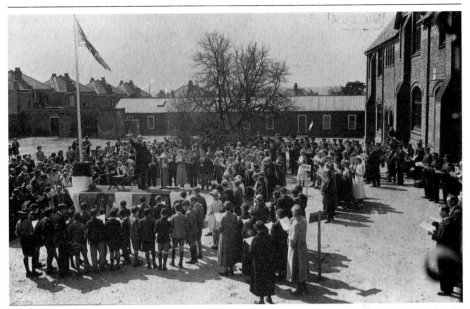

Chas. Harris, organist and choirmaster at Wood Street Congregational church, conducting a choral festival for George V's Jubilee, 1935, in the playground at Queen Elizabeth's Boys' School.

The Duke of Kent and Viscount Hampden at the opening of the new Queen Elizabeth's Boys' School, Queens Road, 1932.

Bow House, No. 35 Wood Street, restored after the bombing in 1940.

The Victoria Hospital, Wood Street, under camouflage for the Second World War. Later a maternity home, it closed in the mid-1980s.

The opening exhibition of the Barnet Record Society at No. 31 Wood Street, 1928. Then, everyone had an initial. Respectable folk had at least two. This lot had impeccable credentials. Left to right: F.L. Dove, Canon F.A. Overton, C.L. Stevenson, S.H. Widdicombe, B.R. Leftwich. Bertram Leftwich was author, civil servant and librarian, who wrote from No. 2 Park Road to spark off the foundation of the Society with a letter to the *Barnet Press*. Sydney Widdicombe wrote local history. Charles Stevenson was a timber merchant who became first curator of the Museum. Frederick Overton was rector of East Barnet. Fred Dove built churches.

Cottages in Wood Street, *c.* 1890. Those above have been demolished to make way for Gillings Court, a pleasant domestic development, with a path to Union Street. No. 32, extreme right, lower picture was F. Eyers, general store, and is now a charming private house.

Eleanor Palmer Almshouses, Wood Street, October 1929. The residents, with Mrs de Bockporter, Trustee, and friend, presumably the man in the cap. Eleanor Palmer was the daughter of the Treasurer to Henry VII.

Elizabeth Allen School at the top of Hillside Gardens. After July 1973 it became a centre for adult education. It now provides sheltered accommodation.

An engraving of the old Congregational church, Wood Street as rebuilt in 1824. The present building dates from 1893.

Congregational church Sunday school outing in 1896.

Ravenscroft Park, *c.* 1880, with Wood Street in background. The pond was sunk in 1890 but drained in 1992. The park is named after James Ravenscroft, a local benefactor.

The old physic well, off Wellhouse Lane (twice visited by Pepys), at its reopening in 1932. The present mock-Tudor building was erected over it in 1937.

Swans on Ravenscroft Park pond, *c.* 1905.

Shops in Wood Street, opposite the park, possibly at the time of George V's coronation, 1911.

Barnet Workhouse, West End Lane, decorated for Edward VII's coronation in 1902.

Wood Street at the junction of King's Road, *c.* 1900. The house is now heavily protected by fences and foliage, no doubt to muffle the noise of traffic.

Barnet Steam Laundry and Holland House, part of the industrial hinterland at the foot of Queen's Road. Both buildings are extant.

Opposite: William John Fry (1825–1900), aged 73. He was bailiff of Whitings Hill Farm, Bell's Hill, and was known as The Hermit of Barnet because he was hirsute. Collecting weapons was his hobby; he walked about with a brace of pistols and swords stuck in his belt.

Watson's optical works, Bell's Hill, showing lenses being ground by hand, *c.* 1910. Watson's made microscopes and other precision instruments including lenses for early TV cameras. The works were damaged by bombing during the Second World War and subsequently merged with the Philips group. A permanent record of their achievements is in the Barnet Museum.

Geoffrey Smith demonstrating a microscope at Watson's. He was formerly a well-known salesman with C.J. Motors, on the edge of Hadley Green, now a pizza house.

Barnet Hospital Carnival, 1921, in fields off Wellhouse Lane, now the extension car park for visitors. The Radio Society was raising money for equipment for patients.

Barnet Road, Arkley, near Glebe Lane, 1911.

Arkley Mill restored in 1930. The ponds were formed when clay was extracted for brick making.

Mr Jones's brick field at Arkley, 1890. He was in business until the First World War.

Fold Farm, Galley Lane, Arkley on the site of James Ravenscroft's moated seventeenth-century farm. The moat is still there. This is great riding-school country.

Diamond Jubilee celebrations in 1897 at the Gate Inn at Arkley. The gate was not for tolls but to prevent cattle straying.

The windmill at Arkley, 1895 (compare with p. 90).

SECTION FIVE

The Hadleys

There are five Hadleys: the Green, immediately beyond Barnet High Street, leading to the Highstone, and, to the east of them, Monken Hadley, the Common and the Wood. This enchanting study, where Green meets Highstone, was taken by Lambert Matthews of the Lyonsdown Amateur Photographic Association in July 1895. The post office and old Windmill Inn are in the background.

Hadley Hurst, on the Common, 1937. Probably the heady climax of a Conservative Party fête.

Horse play at another fête at Hadley House, on the Green, 7 July 1934.

Hawkins's cart yard on Hadley Green adjoining his house in Dury Road, after 1895. His house and extension border the goose pond in which a set of cart wheels can be seen. The rims were soaked to make them swell.

Hadley Brewery on the Green, 1934. Brewing ceased after the Second World War and the building was demolished in the late 1970s.

This dray delivered daily to local pubs. There was a second brewery behind the Two Brewers, hence its name.

A group of old vehicles arranged like a still life beside what had been Hawkins's house, July 1935. The vehicle on the left was Barnet's second fire engine, purchased in 1862. The owner was ordered to remove them from the Green.

A late Edwardian outing to the rebuilt Old Windmill Inn. Buses ran between here and the tube at Golders Green.

A private, or pirate, bus outside the Two Brewers, c. 1925–6. The driver was a Mr Case.

This horse-bus plied between Hadley and Whetstone long before 1907 when the tube reached Golders Green.

The rebuilt Two Brewers in 1934. Note the circular AA destination board on the fence. The pub was demolished in 1992.

Gothic Place, Dury Road, *c.* 1890. Not much changed today.

Post office, Hadley Highstone, *c.* 1925. Next to it is a cobblers. Both have gone, and Hadley Green Garage which succeeded them is now closed.

Servants at the large houses on the Green and Common probably lived in these cottages at the Highstone. Built about 1870 they were photographed in 1958 when designated as part of a clearance area.

The Old Windmill, *c.* 1890–5. It was rebuilt in 1899.

Old cottages behind the Windmill in 1934. Apparently they were used as a guest house kept by one Mrs Wilsher whose notice proclaims, 'The Travellers Rest. Good Lodgings'. Note the water butt.

Hadley Highstone, 1898, photographed by E.A. Maxwell of High Street, Barnet. The Highstone was erected in about 1740 to mark the spot where the Earl of Warwick was supposedly killed at the Battle of Barnet, fought on Easter Monday 1471. Fog played an important role in the outcome of that battle. Today fog tends to linger over the Green and Highstone longer than elsewhere. The monument was removed to its present position to facilitate road improvements. The old Great North Road is to the right of it; Kitts End Road, a more ancient route, to the left.

Miss Samuels, daughter of the church warden of Monken Hadley, and friend, *c.* 1880. Taken from the Old Forge. On the left is the old track to Kitts End which passes Pymlico House where, enclosed in the oft restored residence, is evidence of a sixteenth-century

cottage. On the right is the road across Hadley Green. Did this lovely composition inspire the similar scene on page 93?

Boy Scouts building a bonfire on Hadley Green for the coronation of George VI, 1937. The site seems to be on the west side of the Great North Road with Hadley Green Road in the background.

Opposite, above: Smith's Lane, near the Two Brewers. The forge is to the right of the oddly shaped weather-boarded building.

Opposite, below: Elm House, Hadley Green, in the 1930s. It was destroyed by bombs during the Second World War. The land is now public with a path to New Barnet.

The Priory, Monken Hadley, which was taken down in the 1960s. Ecclesiastically it was an outpost of Saffron Walden and was originally called South Wood. In the background is the church of St Mary, dating from the late fifteenth century. On its tower is a copper beacon, part of a nationwide network lit to warn of perils such as the Spanish Armada. It was ignited in the summer of 1988, for the four hundredth anniversary of that Spanish mishap.

Opposite, above: The Barnet Record Society, which visited Monken Hadley *en masse* in 1934 seen at the Priory.

Opposite, below: Mr B.R. Leftwich, co-founder, addressing members, only one of whom is hatless. The bus in the background was probably chartered. This was not a scheduled route and piracy had ended.

St Mary's, Monken Hadley, *c.* 1900, when its superb architecture was hidden by pestiferous ivy, removed in 1916.

The Gate House, with the vicarage visible behind it, and, on the right, Hadley Lodge which was gutted by fire in 1981.

The Hermitage, next to Hadley Lodge, was demolished in the winter of 1872/3. The tree in the foreground is known as Warwick's Oak. It was uprooted by soldiers as a prank in 1865, and then replanted roots upward.

One of four gates to Hadley Common erected to prevent cattle roaming. The elderly man at the gatehouse on Camlet Way is keeper Mr Foames, around 1930. The gates remain except when motorists knock them down, but are permanently open even though the right to graze cattle (as below in 1910) is still valid. It is a liberty which has not been exercised in recent years.

Gladsmuir, Hadley Common, 1951, since when it has been severely damaged by fire but rebuilt much as it was. Its ancient name of Lemmons was revived when Kingsley Amis and Elizabeth Jane Howard lived here in the 1970s. Their guest, the poet laureate Cecil Day-Lewis, died at Lemmons in 1972. The next owners reverted to the name Gladsmuir.

Hadley Common early in the twentieth century. The house on the right of Hurst Cottage was called Bolena. It has since been replaced.

Near Hadley Wood bridge, 1952. The train carrying the body of George VI from Sandringham to King's Cross. Was the trespassing crowd hoping to have a sight of the coffin?

East Barnet, New Barnet

Cat Hill, 1902, with the bridge over the Pymmes brook. Up to the right was the ancient Cat Inn, burned down in 1955. The site is now a supermarket for frozen meat.

East Barnet village about 1895 when there was a sort of village green where the war memorial later stood. Jackson Road is in the background.

Flood at Brookhill Road in April 1878.

Cat Hill from the Cockfosters direction, early 1920s.

Clock House Parade, partly on the site of the house after which it is named, 1957. The parade was built in 1926 and the clock tower from the house was retained. Presumably this photograph was taken on a Sunday or early closing day. All of the shops have since changed hands. What a fall out of Williams Brothers!

The original clock house was built in the early sixteenth century. Its successor, seen here, was demolished in 1925.

There were many gentlemen's estates in East Barnet. This one, Oak Hill House, was on land known as Le Monkefrith. It now belongs to a theological training college.

The west frontage of Osidge House, the early nineteenth-century mansion once the home of Sir Thomas Lipton. It lies off Chase Side and is now a home for retired nurses.

Boys' Farm Home, East Barnet: staff houses. This was founded by Lt Col. Gillum to help orphaned boys of good character. It stands close to the parish church of St Mary (below).

The tomb on the extreme left was erected about 1775, and a vestry was built on the west side reaching to the tomb in 1816. According to Pevsner the nave walls and three small windows are Norman.

Probably the lodge of Trevor Hall, Church Hill Road, *c.* 1935. One much be-gabled wing remains.

Church Hill Road in the 1930s. The pond has since been drained and the land forms part of Oak Hill Park.

Church Hill Road leading to Osidge, 1955. In the last forty years the road has been widened and vegetation on either side has been cut down. A country lane has become almost a main artery.

Opposite, above: Vernon's Pig Farm during the First World War when this type of farming was encouraged to ease the food shortage. It was on the site of Southaw School, Russell Lane, now part of Barnet College.

Opposite, below: Mr Gould & Son, who traded in Union Street, with their fish and game cart by the lych gate of East Barnet church.

The sewerage farm in Brunswick Park Road, 1910, between the present public library and the cemetery.

The opening of Oak Hill Park, 1931, by Viscount Hampden, Lord Lieutenant of Hertfordshire.

Mr Barker at his shop at Preston Cottages, East Barnet Road, near the present Sainsburys. He was a founder member of the Barnet Cycling Club.

Oak Hill Park in the early thirties.

The National School, Church Hill Road, September 1952, shortly before its demolition. Built in 1863, it was East Barnet's first village school.

Lyonsdown Road, 6 April 1886. The house was called The Chestnuts; the photo was by F. Crosbie, honorary secretary of the Lyonsdown Photographic Society, whose family lived there.

Mr Clarke, with sons Robert and William, ouside their cottage at the bottom of Cat Hill, *c.* 1900. Note the bird cages, probably imprisoning linnets.

East Barnet Fire Brigade, 1903, at Leicester Road station, only recently vacated for more conveniently situated premises at the west end of Station Road. Firemen here are standing, with their Chief Officer Captain Henry York, around their new Shand Mason horse-drawn carriage.

Proclamation of accession of Queen Elizabeth II at East Barnet Town Hall, 1952, with the high sheriff of Hertfordshire, Councillor Cyril Jordan and Vivian Joyce, town clerk.

Members of the last East Barnet Urban District Council in the Town Hall garden, 14 June 1964.

East Barnet Town Hall and urban district council offices in 1958. These handsome municipal buildings are now doomed, with most windows boarded up and many trees felled. There was proud rivalry between the Barnets. In their heyday East certainly had the

finer Town Hall (see p. 69 for Chipping's) though Friern Barnet, outside the scope of this book, is architecturally pleasing in a different, 1940s, style. All three are now part of the Greater London Borough of Barnet, with headquarters in Hendon of all places.

East Barnet loved its carnivals. They manifested a civic pride which has been downgraded, in terms of showmanship and local initiative, by the regrettable move towards central government. Here, at Whitsun 1954, Councillor D.J.R. Howell, chairman of the council, on horseback, salutes Mayor Herbert Patrick. Note the small boys in short trousers not jeans.

Traders' Carnival, 1948, passing the Baptist church in Station Road, since demolished. This was in the immediate post-war era when comparatively few vehicles were on the roads and there was still rationing.

The 1949 Carnival on Whit Monday. The costumes worn almost certainly represent a triumph of individual ingenuity born of wartime exhortations to 'make do and mend'. Austerity was still necessary.

Mrs Montague Main and two correctly dressed schoolboys eye each other's headgear without envy. (Who will have the best bag of zebras?)

Long Street, New Barnet, before reconstruction in 1930. It is now busy Longmore Avenue, a cut through to Enfield from the Great North Road.

East Barnet Road, 1954. The buildings on the right have all been redeveloped as part of the Sainsburys site and another adjoining it.

East Barnet Road from Victoria Road, *c.* 1926. Note the advertisement above Gristwood's as agents for Achille Serre, then a famous name in dry cleaning. The offices of the *Barnet Press* are now in this redeveloped block.

Junction of East Barnet and Lytton Roads, probably pre-1914. The right-hand side is largely unaltered.

The railway bridge over East Barnet Road was reconstructed in 1936 to allow clearance for double-decker buses. Note that the porticoed entrance to New Barnet station had not then been removed.

Classroom at Margaret Road School, 1926 (above). The future author and broadcaster Edward Blishen is third from left, fourth row. His several volumes of autobiography refer, thinly disguised, to Barnet, where he grew up, and to Hadley Wood, where he has lived for most of his adult life.

Edward (left), aged 11, in his rugger togs at the family home in Manor Road, off Wood Street. He was a pupil at Queen Elizabeth's Boys' School.

Playground at Margaret Road, *c.* 1934. Charles Rice, son of the nurseryman below, is third from the left, front row.

L.T. Rice, garden contractor, with his float at a carnival held between the wars.

A party of women and children from St Giles Mission in London's East End on a visit to Folly Farm, by Hadley Wood, in July 1933. By custom children from Cromer Road School, New Barnet, presented them with flowers. The visitors appear to be cordoned off from their well-wishers.

International Stores, East Barnet Road, 1917. The unfortunate male assistants had gone to the Front.

War

New Barnet station approach on York Road at the turn of the century. Men of the North Hertfordshire Yeomanry are off to the Boer War. Where most of the crowd are standing is now a car park and bus terminus. The gardens on the right became a site for flats in the 1930s. The station portico was removed in the 1960s but a replacement, higher up the slope, was constructed in 1993.

Mafeking Day – as opposed to night – celebrations, May 1900. Above, at the King of Prussia, Barnet High Street; below, at the junction of New (St Albans) Road and High Street. No doubt it livened up later.

Army cadets of the 12th Middlesex Volunteers at the Range, Manor House, Hadley, in 1863.

Members of the Royal Engineers, Barnet Detachment, 1917.

High Barnet Troop 224, Rangers, who perhaps served as first aiders, or nursing auxiliaries, in the First World War.

East Barnet church hall in use as a war hospital, 1916. The patients seated beside, not in, their beds look ominously ripe for return to the carnage.

Postwomen of the First World War.

Ewen Hall, Wood Street, June 1915. A concert both for and by wounded soldiers.

General Lord Byng, of Vimy, unveiling the memorial to Barnet's 246 dead in the First World War on 3 April 1921.

East Barnet's war memorial (since removed to a position beside the road) being unveiled on 27 June 1920, Canon Overton officiating.

Bomb damage at No. 144 Crescent Road,
New Barnet, 1941. The house was said not
to be beyond repair.

Mrs George Bozier rescuing her pets
and some belongings.

Bombing at Wood Street, 18 October 1940. The Barnet Museum and Bow House were among the buildings wrecked.

On the opposite side of the street this terrace was partly destroyed. Note, today, how well it was restored.

Havoc wrought by a parachute mine in Bell's Hill on 6 November 1940. There were 17 killed, 31 injured.

Belgian soldiers, rescued from the Dunkirk beaches, at High Barnet station on 1 June 1940.

East Barnet police firing the air raid warning maroon, as a training exercise, in 1917. Left to right: Sgt C. Key, Mr Stevens, PC Street, PC Sadler.

Civil Defence personnel of East Barnet at Church Farm, May 1954. Ready to cope with the nuclear age, or reluctant to forego wartime camaraderie? A little of each perhaps.

Sport and Customs

Beating the bounds at East Barnet, 1933. Mr Walter Stutters is literally having the boundary impressed on his head. The purpose of this old ceremony was to make citizens, and especially children, familiar with the borders of their parish. On the extreme right is Stanley Kipping, a *Barnet Press* reporter.

The bounds being beaten beside the railway at East Barnet, 1920.

Mr G. Keyworth, Chairman of Barnet Urban District Council, about to be beaten.
Councillor Hewes is on his right, *c.* 1925.

In 1920 the bounds were also beaten beside the Pymmes brook at Cat Hill. On the bridge are the Revd Arnold Overton, Theo Keynes (organist), Captain Ralston, Alan Cobden and historian S.H. Widdicombe.

Before the ceremony at Old Court Pleasure Gardens, Wood Street.

MR. BOYES
2 DAUGHTERS (?)

SEARLE (?)

JACK
PICKUP (?)

HUGH
WILLIAMS (?)

MR. A.S. MAYES
(?)

MR. GEORGE
MALINS

The Arkley Range was near Barnet Gate Wood.

The Old Elizabethans cricket team, 1923. All were, or should have been, ex-pupils of Queen Elizabeth's Boys' School.

Golf players on Sunset Fields, Old Folk Manor, 1897.

Barnet Bowling Club (Captain: F. Wood) at Clifford Road, New Barnet, 1933.

Barnet Football Club, 1894–5, with non-playing swells in attendance.

Amateur cup winners, 1945–6. The club is now professional.

Barnet United, winners of the Herts Benevolent Shield, 1935–6. Left to right, back row: D. Foster (trainer), H. Winchester (Hon. Sec.), C. Robertson, G. Reed, E. Capell (Captain), E.W. Lambert, H. Bodger. Centre row: H. Easton, E. Beer, L. Dennis, H. Yendall, R. Dennis, C. Woods. Front row: H. Grimwade, G.M. Shears.

Lester Finch, Barnet's international footballer in 1935. His memoirs are available at the Barnet Museum.